**Patrick Cox**

CUTTING EDGE

TAMASIN DOE

# Patrick Cox

## Wit, Irony and Footwear

Thames and Hudson

First published in Great Britain
in 1998 by Thames and Hudson Ltd, London

Design copyright © 1998 The Ivy Press

Text copyright © 1998 Tamasin Doe

British Library Cataloguing-in-Publication Data

A catalogue record for this book is
available from the British Library

ISBN 0-500-01858-8

Printed in Hong Kong

*Opposite: python sandal,
spring/summer 1998.*

# Contents

This isn't a job for me — it's an obsession. I hope that one thing people get from my shoes is a sense of fun. I love what I do, I love the craft of shoe-making. I want to celebrate its traditions at the same time as I push forward the boundaries. And the best — indeed only — way I know of doing that is to make a product that people will get a buzz out of using. I'm into instant gratification. Nobody could ever say I was a snob. I love all types of shoes, from sneakers to stilettos. But that's also the times we're living in: a modern mix of comfort and contradiction. Isn't it wild that a shoe can say all that?

Patrick Cox

**P**ATRICK COX is a living contradiction. He is the shoe designer who has shod a million people in his everyday Wannabe loafer at the same time as giving us sublime satin slippers; he is the businessman who has developed his name into a premium brand (without need of a bank loan or backer) while maintaining the rollicking air of what he calls 'a living cartoon', with a wicked machine-gun laugh that strafes the room every two minutes. When he describes how he arrived here, with two London shops, countless outlets around the world and an output of 350,000 pairs of shoes every year, Cox also manages to sound as though his was a level-headed life plan – albeit one reached after a somewhat chaotic, and lucky, journey.

It is these contradictions that make Cox different. His creativity as a designer is counterpointed with the clinical realism of a banker. It meant that while the rest of the world was fighting an arduous recession in the early Nineties, Cox was searching for a way to build his name into a global brand. And he has done. Certainly his fashion-forward shoes have been worn by Madonna and every member of entertainment's royal family, but he also wanted to define a shoe which could become a meritocratic style worn by everyone: from the wealthy executive to a teenager shopping for his or her first pair of proper shoes. Thus the Wannabe was born in 1993 and Cox's career became turbo-charged, thrusting him from being an in-the-know designer who produced beautiful shoes for the elite to the status of an international brand. He is now learning to live with the fact that his name is no longer his own. He is a label; but more than that his moniker has become generic. In the Marches, the Italian Adriatic region devoted to shoe manufacture, 'Il Wannabe' has nothing to do with the products of a 35-year-old Canadian; it refers to the modern loafer, pure and simple.

Cox has an animated, excited manner. Rather than talking, he raps at 100 mph and illustrates his points with wild, descriptive hand gestures and a barely disguised smile, especially when he is talking about the day Wannabe refuelled his career. 'I knew the day of the "cute" shoe designer was over,' he says. 'Brand is everything. Breaking through the sale of 2,000 pairs was so important for me. After that I headed for 20,000, then 100,000.' By way of explaining his main influences, Cox says that he venerates the dynastic Italian leather companies. He may not yet be a Gucci, Ferragamo or Prada, but in the first ten years of his business he has come to out-sell a number of the companies he admires.

In many ways the shoe industry is lucky to have Patrick Cox. As a child, he lived a peripatetic life. Travelling the world with his Canadian mother, Maureen, he followed his English father, Terry, a languages academic, from Edmonton to postings in Nigeria,

'I started my business from home, designing, producing and selling shoes. When you pay for your mistakes, as I did, you learn that you have to make it work.'

*Patrick Cox and Helena Christensen shoot the Wannabe advertising campaign, spring/summer 1996.*

8

Chad, Cameroon and back again. It left him with an acculturation instinct which inhibited him from settling into the veterinary career that, as an A-grade student majoring in the sciences, was his expected course. He laughs, 'If I came home with 95 per cent in a test we'd have a family discussion about what happened to the other five per cent… my best subjects were chemistry, biology and math – I hated subjective classes like art where the teacher could tell me I was wrong but not show why.' Even today Cox doesn't sketch. When he designs it is a mental process which culminates in a working drawing, accurate to the millimetre.

'Designing was never even considered a career option,' says Cox. 'I loved school but finished a year early to speed things up… I was bored.' He moved to Toronto and immersed himself in the club sub-culture, working the door at the In club. 'It was a start,' he says, 'but it was a city where you were convinced that things were happening on the other side of the world. There were always dreams of escape.' That dream destination changed depending on where the best music, and therefore the best fashion, was being made. In 1976 the dream was London to live Punk; in 1978 it was New York to ride the New Wave; then it was back to London again in 1981 to become a Blitz Kid.

At the age of 19 Cox produced his first pair of shoes. They were Mao slippers customized into boots for Toronto-based designer Loucas Kleanthous. Realizing that Cox had a gift for shoe design, Kleanthous encouraged Cox to move to London to take a course at Cordwainers Technical College. On a reconnaissance trip to London in the spring of 1983, Cox met club promoter Rusty Egan's girlfriend, Hayley, on the Kings Road. They kept in touch, and when he returned in September to take up his place at Cordwainers, Cox moved in with the pair at 9 Chapel Street, Belgravia. It placed him at the heart of the fashion and music scene, and gave him access to the designers who would later break his career on the London catwalks.

## Serious fun

Cox's business acumen and ability to find himself in the right place at the right time are still matched by his determination to enjoy his work. He is and always has been a notorious party animal. One friend remembers a 'fine performance' when he 'vogued' in a Thai restaurant in Paris; while during the selling season, at shoe fairs in Paris, New York and Düsseldorf, he famously holds parties every night. Cox balks at intellectualizing any aspect of his work, even to the buyers who expect a little pretentious navel-gazing from designers. But his success has its foundations rooted in a serious corner of his personality. In the mid-Eighties, despite the wild night-time partying, he spent the days labouring

*The Wannabe spring/summer 1997 campaign, inspired by the film* Casino.

over his work. He says, 'I started my business from home, design-ing, producing and selling shoes. When you pay for your mistakes, as I did, you learn that you have to make it work.'

These disparate elements to Cox's make-up are reflected in his two Chelsea shops. At No. 8 Symons Street, just off Sloane Square, the Patrick Cox mainline collections are sold in a shop which has the patrician atmosphere of a National Trust parlour. Slick stilettos, cut from vivid silks, and highly polished boots rest on antique furniture. His clientele discuss their requirements from an elegant banquette as staff move silently across the coir floor. Gravitas hangs heavy in the air and there is a conspicuous absence of the cosmetic cheeriness taught on customer relations courses.

Around the corner, on Sloane Street, Patrick Cox shows his other face in the windows of a second store, this time devoted to speed, youth and modernity. Mannequins shod in funky, clunky Wannabe loafers front a twenty-first-century interior. Also displayed are this month's clothes and accessories, all sold under the Cox label.

It's this combination which has allowed Cox to travel further than any other independent shoe designer of his generation. It also does nothing to disturb the impression that Patrick Cox is on a mission to give Britain its own successful leather goods company to rival those housed on the via della Spiga in Milan. If he can do

it on the lower reaches of Sloane Street, which until the opening of the Cox outlets had encountered nothing more radical than the tread of well-heeled green wellingtons, he can probably do it anywhere in the world.

## Traditional values

Cox chose Chelsea as his commercial home exactly because he did not want to become a member of the fashionable London elite (then centred around Soho) and run the risk of stamping a sell-by date on his own career. Instead, he chose to sit outside the clique. He settled into Chelsea, rarely attends fashion parties and never courts society. When Symons Street, his first shop, opened opposite Peter Jones – a department store proud of its credentials as a bastion of the Chelsea set – the company still employed just Cox and an assistant. The shop opened during a recession and was designed to symbolize a new seriousness in his attitude. Cox said at the time, 'My shoes have always been in clothing stores, where there's usually loud music, a young clientele and not really any room to sit and take your time. I wanted an old-fashioned salon where customers would feel pampered, where they could hang around for a while if they felt like it.'

The stock was as deliberately unusual as the store concept; shoes were to be sold alongside antiques, and an Empire chair

'We throw our ideas away every six months because the newest shoe must always look wrong, ahead of its time.'

could be bought in the same transaction as a pair of cuffed boots. As it turned out, this was just as well; the first shipment of shoes arrived two weeks late and for a fortnight Cox was selling antiques instead of shoes. In any case he had no proof that when the shoes did arrive, the demi-monde would appear on his doorstep to buy them. He says of that period, 'I thanked God every day for Peter Jones. I still do. Every customer who came here for the first few months was carrying a new mop; they'd come out of Peter Jones and say, like, "ooh what is that little place?"' Their interest was an unexpected addition to his fashionable client base, although on reflection not an entirely surprising one. Cox had always prided himself on his traditional English shoe-making values. To this day his proudest moments are when he sells a pair of shoes to a City gent who would normally order his shoes from John Lobb Ltd of St James's. 'It reminds me that my shoes aren't only fashionable. They're good.'

The English tradition of shoe-making has been a profound influence. Being an unwavering perfectionist, Cox is as interested in the way a shoe is made as the way it looks. He will dissect its construction as though it were a veterinary specimen. The point of English manufacture is a certain pride in the triumph of quality over style. Talking about men's shoes, Cox says, 'In England there's something suspect about a light shoe, and I myself prefer a solid, substantive style. When it comes to making up my shoes in Italy there's always this assumption that I'm actually looking for a finer look than I am – sometimes it takes a lot to explain that I really do want a shoe that's heavy… There's a kind of prehistoric pleasure to be had from a good piece of hide.'

Cox is fascinated by traditional craft skills. 'It's endless, what you can do with a piece of leather. Polishing, embellishing, buffing; you should be able to turn a good man's shoe over and see your reflection in the sole… The act of traditional shoe-making certainly has a lot to do with gender. Men carry out the cutting, women always stitch, men form the shoe and women always work on the finishing. It's very masculine, and very sexist – which may explain why so many shoe designers are men.'

## The design process

Inscribed on a few pages of Patrick Cox's Filofax is information that is worth millions. The small, tight, hand-printed letters spell out various abstract descriptions which, within five months, will be applied to at least 175,000 pairs of shoes – one season's work for Patrick Cox.

Because he doesn't think in terms of paper visuals, the information is also stored as mental snapshots, memories – sometimes invented ones – of what a TV star wore or heel shapes that are yet

*Opposite: 'Mondrian' shoe from spring/summer 1995; and the Patrick Cox store in Singapore, opened in 1997. Left: where it all begins – Cox's Filofax, filled with the ideas that will become next year's shoes.*

to be invented. The approach, to quote Cox's own words, is 'anally methodical'. He explains: 'The design process for the next season doesn't even begin until I've spent myself on the previous season. Throughout selling, I edit all day. I throw the shoes around, end up hating some of them and basically exhaust myself… I'm my worst critic.' To recover, Cox takes time out for three weeks, although during that period he visits clients in the Far East as well as holidaying in Bali. Only then does he concentrate on the next six months.

Rewinding, Cox goes on to describe the initial decisions on colours and finishes which must be finalized before the footwear takes shape. Eighteen months before the launch of a collection he visits a tannery in Italy where some of the leather designs will be exclusive to him for a season. The designing itself begins a year in advance. Cox travels with his notes to Italy to work with his assistant, Fabrizio Viti. They visit Renzo at Formificio Romagnolo, last-maker for Wannabe, PCs and the men's collection. There are no sketches; Renzo files away at the last, listening to Cox's directions. 'I'll say, "Remember that shape I like, but it needs to be pointier." He files, we assess, he files… The end result is more like a piece of sculpture.'

Cox is reverential about the craftsmen he works with. He believes, as Thomas Carlyle put it, that 'a man cannot make a pair of shoes rightly unless he do it in a devout style.' The shoes themselves may have a humorous or frivolous charm, but Cox also believes that the art of cobbling nonpareil begins with meticulous craftsmanship, and ends with hand-finishing. He says, 'Shoes are a craft more than anything else. In Italy they don't use the term "designer" in manufacturing circles.' If Cox has one problem with design courses today it's their overproduction of designers, leaving too few craftsmen to care for the process.

Cox is regarded as an oddity in the Marches. Few designers become so involved in the production process. 'Ferdinando, my ladies' heel-maker at Tacchificio Corva, lets me work with him. By only working in 2-D you lose something. I want to be there as he files and the heel takes shape… If two people work together it stimulates ideas. There is an incredible level of respect. It's a dialogue with the people who are making my work happen. I listen to them, and my contacts with these craftsmen have turned into personal relationships.'

Decisions and fit trials are completed on the men's and Wannabe ranges first. Designing for both is a matter of restraint and nuance. With the women's collection, however, every season is what Cox calls 'revolution rather than evolution'. He maintains that 'designing for women has nothing to do with respecting tradition. We throw our ideas away every six months because the

*Paul Weller wearing snakeskin by Cox.*

*The Patrick Cox campaign for spring/summer 1997.*

newest shoe initially looks almost wrong, ahead of its time. It needs to take a few months to become understood – after all, it's sold to the buyers a full six months before it reaches the shops, and fashion moves fast. Really fast.'

Once the lasts and heels are decided, Viti and Cox annexe themselves at his Sixties beach apartment in Civitanova. Together they work intensively from 8am to midnight, sketching over a background of loud music which Cox calls his 'food'. During these weeks, the creator within Cox dominates and nothing is allowed to upset his equilibrium. He describes how people misconstrue the megawatt sound of Donna Summer and squeals of laughter: 'Our new managing director was there one time and he kept coming in the room thinking we were having a party. We'd just growl at him – the music is what makes it happen. Designing is so subjective, you have to be in the right mood.'

Because Cox tends to draw on his observations from TV or music, pundits sometimes assume that Cox is using an actual historical heel or Seventies leather finish. But although he may well evoke a memory of what Farrah Fawcett might have worn in an episode of Charlie's Angels, there is no literal connection. He is trying to define a mood rather than replicate it. After several weeks Cox and Viti emerge with working drawings that detail every stitch and measure every centimetre. Asked whether he works to a shoe quota, he says, 'We don't count the styles, we simply work until I figure we've got a collection together.' The samples are then made up, and fit trials can begin.

Patrick Cox is a perfect sample size eight and hasn't worn anyone else's shoes since he graduated from college in 1985. Therefore it is fair to say that his men's collections are designed for him – the fit trials are also carried out on Cox's own feet. 'If I ask the question, "Would I wear it?", and the answer is "No", it doesn't go into the collection. That goes for both design and fit.'

Comfort is paramount and Cox applies the same emphasis to his women's collections. Just as Salvatore Ferragamo was horrified by the mutilations that footwear could inflict, and determined to improve the situation, Cox does not believe in the agonies of fashion. Heels that displace balance and call for uncomfortable posture correction, or toes that cramp and pinch to achieve a spear-like elegance, are to him unacceptable concessions. In pursuit of comfort, the female fit trials are carried out on two very different workers from the factory: one with a svelte model's proportions, the other with a very real figure and weight. In the end such crafted comfort must be paid for – at around £100 to £650 for shoes and boots in the mainline collections – but in turn, function is happily married to aesthetic. Cox feels that should be every designer's grail.

*'Very Farrah Fawcett', the creamy fold-down boot for autumn/winter 1997.*

'If I ask the question, "Would I wear it?", and the answer is "No", it doesn't go into the collection.'

13

**C**OX CALLS HIMSELF a control freak but it was his collaboration with designers that put his shoes on catwalks – at eye-level with every important designer, fashion editor and pop star. Talking about those first collections, Cox says, 'I'm not a team player but early in my career it was useful to be around other people, bouncing ideas off them.' Often it also meant having to fund his own work, especially with the smaller, newer fashion designers who attract important media attention. For Cox, his work for Vivienne Westwood, John Galliano, John Flett and Anna Sui was to be his springboard into business.

In 1983, when London clubland was the axis around which the music and fashion worlds circled, clothes were the measure of a person. Those who didn't make the effort to enter into the costume fantasy were left outside on the pavement, unable to get past the door staff who were de facto style police. It was at one such club, the Pink Pussy, that Cox was invited into the inner sanctum of Vivienne Westwood's entourage when he was spotted by staff from her World's End and Nostalgia of Mud shops. They recognized him and liked the cut of his outfit, so they asked him if he wanted to hang with them. It may sound puerile today, but at the time it was an invitation to mix with a cool

*Inset: Vivienne Westwood catwalk, Paris, 1984.*

elite of fashion designers and stars. Cox was to meet Westwood, who went on to become a valuable patron.

In 1984, just three weeks before her March show, Westwood asked Cox to provide shoes for her 'Clint Eastwood' collection, which was to be shown in a courtyard at the Louvre in Paris. Cox traipsed over to France by train and ferry with his sample bag. His assortment of handmade samples included a pair that had not been requested: knotted gold leather mules. Cox knew they were a risk – at a time when the accepted style kept feet flat on the ground, the sole was a mighty platform.

Westwood's reaction when she saw the shoes – 'How hideous, how Seventies' – could hardly be described as enthusiastic. But events took an unpredictable turn. 'On the day of the show, we watched the clothes truck arrive. What we actually got was a few completed outfits, a pile of sewing machines and the rest of the collection pinned to rolls of fabric… The Italians [manufacturers] hadn't finished the collection… We were sent into the audience to find Stephen Jones [milliner] and Stephen Linard [designer], in fact just about anybody who could sew, to bring them backstage and get them working.'

With minutes to go, the 'Clint Eastwood' collection was still in production and the backstage area was 'utter, utter chaos, with everyone fighting and bitching'. At that point, Cox was

PATENT PLATFORM
For Vivienne Westwood, 1984

**Cox suggested the rounded sole and patent finish on this early platform, which features an extended tongue lapping from an ankle strap.**

## GOLD PLATFORM
For Vivienne Westwood, 1984

**Fate was on Cox's side when disaster struck Westwood's Paris show, and platforms went on to become a Vivienne Westwood mainstay.**

## SUEDE WEDGE
For John Galliano, 1987

**A low suede pump is embellished with a ruched cotton ankle strap.**

## 'BROKEN HEEL DOLLY SHOE'
For John Flett, 1986

**The carved wooden heel was designed to conjure up the image of 'a working girl staggering home from her night of labour on the streets'.**

In a parody of a tramp's boot, ticking cotton peels away from the heel. Galliano nevertheless judged the shoes 'too perfect', and sent his models out into the mud to make them look more authentic.

**Cox's backless ghillies for John Flett were a hybrid of the ballet pump, the mule and the sneaker.**

appointed stylist. 'I was like holding up a jacket and skirt, shouting "Does this go?" to anyone who could hear me. In the end we just threw the clothes and shoes in a huge pile in the middle of the floor and told the girls [models] to do it themselves. They all went for the sandals because they were so new. They were actually fighting for them.' The platform went on to become a Westwood mainstay. In 1993 Naomi Campbell famously took a tumble from a nine-inch pair which, in effect, were the great-great granddaughters of Cox's mules.

Cox went on to work with the design partnership Bodymap, while still a student. David Hollah and Stevie Stewart wanted some fringed moccasins in fluorescent orange and green. 'I hand-stitched them at college – my fingers were bleeding because of these bloody moccasins. The shoes sucked up the spray paint until they were stiff with it. Only then did they actually look fluorescent.' As it turned out, those 'bloody moccasins' later became the template for the construction of Wannabes.

John Galliano became another client after he saw Westwood's 'Clint Eastwood' show. His own 'Fallen Angel' collection was styled with plaster — some of it thrown at the audience, the rest decorating the heads and bodies of the models. It was a grungy look, at a muddy venue (a tent at the Duke of York's Barracks on the King's Road). Cox recalls how when Galliano was presented with his too-perfect leather and ticking hobo boots, 'he got somebody to distract me while he sent the models outside to scuff the shoes with mud. When I saw them trooping back I screamed, "What have you done, the shoes are mine, you're not paying for them!" John turned to me and said, "But Patrick, it's designer mud."'

*Inset: John Galliano catwalk, 1986.*

'**W**HY, PEOPLE ASK ME, are Wannabes just so damn comfortable? They don't know about tubular moccasin construction [the leather is wrapped under the foot forming a seamless base], or the fact there's no toe puff or stiffening – they don't need to. All they know is that when they think they've moved on from the Wannabe style, they can't bring themselves to dump them… the biggest compliment comes when I see a really knackered pair of my shoes.'

The loafer has been an enduring signature for Patrick Cox, but it was with the launch of the Wannabe label that it took on a life of its own. In 1995, before the Wannabe loafer was given its own dedicated outlet, Patrick Cox

became a byword for outrageous success. Newspapers sent reporters to stand outside Symons Street with customers who were willing to queue for up to an hour to claim a pair of the sought-after shoes. Delivery men and shop staff were offered bribes to 'lose a pair', and Cox even had to employ a doorman, called Junior. There were just too many people shopping for too few pairs, in a space that was far too small. Wannabe was a gilt-edged phenomenon.

When Cox designs a style he usually accepts that it will have a shelf life of one, possibly two, seasons. But with this 'perfect loafer' – one that conforms to the laws of loafer styling but can cope with subtle alterations according to the evolution of trends – he was not prepared to give up so soon. 'Sales of my more solidly constructed shoes were more difficult during the summer months and I needed to find a lighter, softer shoe.' In 1993 every designer label was trying to find a way of shifting premium goods through the recession. The answer was a secondary line, geared to a younger market and selling the label at up to half the price. Cox wanted, rather than

## UNION JACK' WANNABE
Spring/summer 1996

While everyone else was still waking up to the news that London was 'the coolest city on the planet', Cox had already designed a loafer that said it all.

## CHUNKY CLOG
Spring/summer 1996

A snakeskin loafer is given a heavy clog construction and finished with sturdy rivets. Cox removes the back to create a summer mule.

## SNAKESKIN WANNABE
Spring/summer 1995

'The one and only – beware of imitations,' warns Cox about his best-selling, widely copied loafer. When they came out some customers attempted bribery to lay their hands on a pair.

19

**The Wannabe goes plastic, with a patent upper elevated on a clear gel sole and heel.**

needed, to appeal to this market but didn't want to compromise the basic premise of his mainline collection: quality and comfort.

For all these reasons the loafer was an obvious core style for Cox's new line. Throughout his career he had been using elements from the moccasin loafer, sometimes without consciously acknowledging their provenance. Classic moccasin detailing might be distorted to the point of unrecognizability, as in a lace-up with a welted seam weaving across the toe. At other times he was faithful to the style, as with a sandy beige moccasin desert boot or his white nubuck loafers (featured in the *Face* alongside the instruction, 'to be worn strictly with no socks').

The clincher came in the shape of the zany American actor/comic Pee Wee Herman, a role model who, Cox says, 'was the only person ever to be famous by looking like me and acting like me'. Or rather, it was Herman's ubiquitous footwear, a pair of nerdy white loafers, which inspired the Wannabe range. Cox also found a Sixties photograph of Italian teenagers riding their scooters in high-cut loafers, and the ideas were merged to form his ideal version: broad toe, extended tongue and a toe-caressingly soft construction. Cox says, 'The Wannabe engineering can't be improved on. When I can pick up a pair of shoes, bend them in half and the toe meets the heel, that's when it works for me.'

A name for the new collection was decided early. As a Madonna devotee, Cox not only named his cat after the pop star but was also famous for acting and singing her entire 'Like a Virgin' tour 'to anybody who would watch'. Her fans were called Wannabes (as in want-to-be just like her) and Cox felt it was the right label to stick on a collection that would effectively sell his work to customers who aspired to the mainline collections. 'Everyone was thinking about naff words that masked the purpose of diffusion ranges. Either that or they settled with initials. I didn't think it was an honest method. Wannabe says everything.'

Wannabe's success has gone far beyond the 'junior' market. 'When I look around now, I can't believe that such an anti-statement shoe has had this impact. The entire headquarters of the Gap in San Francisco is staffed by people wearing them. Rei Kawakubo has tons of pairs. The original round-toed Wannabe is still selling 30,000 pairs – five years on!'

In 1995 Cox launched a collection of Wannabe bags and leather goods. In 1998, 50 per cent of total Patrick Cox sales were in the unisex styles of Wannabe loafers. It is a shoe that has single-handedly elevated the average British male expenditure on shoes from £50 to £100 and has been dubbed 'the Doctor Marten of the Nineties'.

### 'WINKLE-PICKER' WANNABE
Autumn/winter 1995

**The sharp treatment: a metal snaffle, inspired by Seventies sunglasses, finishes the pointed Wannabe and gives it an urban feel.**

### 'SOFT' WANNABE
Spring/summer 1998

**The soft treatment: based on a new last, the Wannabe gets a lower, more feminine cut for a lightweight summer loafer.**

SHOE DESIGNERS usually hate training shoes. It is an attitude that hardened through the Nineties as trainers ceased to be used only for sport and came into daily use by armchair athletes. The same thing had happened with the jeans culture of the Seventies. The received wisdom was that, despite their sporty connotations, trainers were a lazy choice.

But Cox acknowledges them as a modern icon. Early on he decided to embrace the sports theme rather than ignore it (after all, until he introduced the PC collection, his own trainers were the only shoes designed by another hand). Elements of his shoe designs – such as their flat, ergonomic styling and broad soles – have always been about activity and Cox has regularly used sporty details. He has borrowed the clip-fastening detail from a ski boot to lend his shoes a modern edge and, in 1986, he designed an exaggerated silver trainer for John Galliano. From the late Eighties his zig-zag soles and striped uppers predicted a wider move towards sportswear.

In 1995 Cox took the theme to its logical conclusion. By introducing PCs, a casual line, he provided an acceptable bridge between pure trainers – which were increasingly looking like scale models of concept cars – and fashion footwear. 'My idea was to do a running shoe, but it had to be an adult running shoe. It's just not cool to wear a wild new Nike that a seven-year-old wants. It was important to do something fashion-friendly, something that isn't always worn with sweat pants... Not a full technical sneaker but something made by a proper running shoe factory.'

PCs are broad in fit and placed on a rubber sole, which is always more comfortable than a leather one. 'I'm a hedonist and I never actually want to be uncomfortable,' says Cox. 'I'm also frenetic, and running shoes are the epitome of North American practicality. I'm not part of the museum culture that puts objects on a pedestal.

'BLOB' SNEAKER
Spring/summer 1998

A fat and funky trainer from the PC range, invented in 1995 to bridge the gap between fashion footwear and big-business trainers. 'My idea was to do a running shoe, but it had to be an adult running shoe. It's just not cool to wear a wild new Nike that a seven-year-old wants.'

Buy them, use them up and dump them is my ethic. I'm not a hoarder; it amazes me that some people can open their wardrobe and have things in there that are 20 years old.' Once again, Cox had identified a niche and filled it. 'You have to watch the ball or you lose sight. PC is about a modern lifestyle, but that doesn't normally mean running the 100 metres.'

Coming from Alberta, where the temperature hits 30 below, one style of performance footwear has always irritated Cox: snowboots. He had long intended to revolutionize the genre, boots at their ugliest but most vital. He is almost breathless as he describes just how ugly they can be and why he felt he owed women this one item: 'The idea behind the moon boot came from one question: "Why does a woman who wears chic dresses at every other moment have to pull on a pair of lurid boots embroidered with snowflakes when she skis?" The answer was, "She shouldn't have to."'

PC LOAFER
Spring/summer 1998

**Bumper-car styling for a piped leather PC. The thick crêpe sole gives it the signature Cox shape.**

PC LACE-UP
Spring/summer 1998

**'PC is about a modern lifestyle, but that doesn't normally mean running the 100 metres.'**

24

# PC's

### PATRICK COX

ADVERTISING
IMAGE
Spring/summer 1996

**The PC top-stitching and crêpe soles both nod towards the feel of a soft suede casual sneaker from the Seventies.**

SNOWBOOT
Autumn/winter 1994

**A luminous, light-refracting silver nylon snowboot designed for modern skiers.**

25

KNOWING HOW TO spot a Patrick Cox shoe is all about understanding the detail. Throughout his career Cox has lent his kooky touch to otherwise traditional shoes. He will extend the tongue of a loafer up the leg until it forms a boot, or cut its back away to form a pair of mules. An i-d bracelet is placed where a snaffle usually sits; a 'modern brogue' is decorated with punching on top of the shoe rather than at the toe; or a classic Oxford is differentiated with a lace that winds its way over the upper instead of bisecting it.

Cox respects the integrity of classic shoe design but he has to have his own say, to make it his own. He says, 'All my designs look like shoes at the end of the day. As a young designer you move the important details all over the place, but with maturity you put them back where they were before, because they look better there. I fight rules all day, but sometimes the continuity makes sense.'

Cox used the process of deconstructing tradition from the outset. His first shoe 'hit' was born of customizing a classic, a tried-and-tested method for street designers who make up in imagination for what they lack in finance and access to production. In 1984, soon after Cox had joined Cordwainers College in Hackney, east London, he saw a construction worker near the college kicking a wall with his steel toe-capped Doctor Marten's boot. 'The toes were really badly scuffed, and the steel toecap had burst through the leather.' Until that time Cox was unaware that the distinctive heavy boots worn by builders and skinheads alike were actually a proper brand name. 'I traced those boots to a shop in Camden

**'WICKED WITCH' MULE**
Spring/summer 1994

**Cox slices off an Oxford at the back and adds a wicked, curvaceous heel.**

OXFORD
Autumn/winter 1997

**A sturdy Oxford exemplifies Patrick Cox's admiration for traditional seaming using pebbled leather.**

### 'PICASSO OXFORD'
Autumn/winter 1987

Cox twists tradition by distorting laces into an asymmetric toe-cap. 'As a young designer you move the important details all over the place...'

### 'PIMP SHOE'
Spring/summer 1997

Square-toed solidity, with detail outlined in white piping.

### WINKLE-PICKER
Autumn/winter 1995

Pointed mock-croc shoes: a modern way with ancient material.

### OXFORD
Autumn/winter 1987

Elasticated gussets are snipped into an otherwise classically styled brogue.

### TRAMLINE LACE-UP
Autumn/winter 1987

Double-laced Oxfords add a subtle design detail beneath a city suit.

and bought a pair of steel-toecapped Dr Marten's shoes to see if I could make them work.' Cox wanted to see if it was possible to create a marketable look by customizing them; and it very definitely was.

The shiny peep-toecaps first appeared on Vivienne Westwood's catwalk on Cox's own feet; he had been asked to model in the show but there were no men's shoes. Cox's inspiration went uncredited, 'but within months I was buying 80 pairs of DMs each week! We were customizing and reselling. We took them to a small cobbler in King's Cross where we could cut away the leather toe and strip the blue paint from the underlying metal.' Each weekend's output was dropped off at Bazaar on South Molton Street, the favoured designer store of pop stars, and had sold out by the following Saturday.

Since then Cox has often applied customization processes, albeit in a less direct manner. His men's and women's shoes still bear the suggestion of a revised classic, although now he is able to dictate every aspect rather than having to work around another company's design. The traditional ghillie, a style of shoe with laces traced up the leg, was recalled by Cox for John Flett's spring 1987 collection. Espadrilles have also been recast, this time as formal shoes. The Mediterranean fisherman's sandals, with their woven rope soles, have been transformed under Cox's hand into elegant high-heeled sling-backs and vertiginous wedges. Using the tradition for a canvas upper, he has applied the fabric to a sharp, structured interpretation of the shape.

### TOECAPPED DM
1984

It started here: the toe-capped Doc Marten launched a shoe empire by dint of Cox's enterprising spirit. Every week he visited a cobbler in King's Cross and stripped the leather skin away from the toe of a quintessential British style. In doing so, he created a fashion icon.

### ESPADRILLE SLING-BACK
Spring/summer 1993

The traditional rope-soled fisherman's sandal is transformed into an up-town shoe.

### HEELED DESERT BOOT
Spring/summer 1993

The classic desert boot is given a fashion profile with raised heel and extended laces.

### BROGUE ANKLE BOOT
Autumn/winter 1996

A modern, chunky boot uses brogue punching and detailing as refinements.

29

UNTIL RECENTLY, 1987 to be exact, Patrick Cox played with dinosaurs. His toy dinosaurs, that is. He stills gets a kick out of visiting Hamley's toy shop 'anytime but Christmas'. He tried bringing his Roger Rabbit doll out of the closet 'but it didn't sit well on the Empire furniture'. Unsurprisingly, Cox has been described as 'the cartoon man'. He adores that interpretation because it captures a childlike element in both his personality and work. When the Symons Street shop opened, the ladies from Peter Jones would refer to Cox as 'that nice young boy who works in the back'. This unstudied demeanour can perplex those who meet him. 'I have an appreciation of that innocence we see in cartoons. I grew up quickly as a child and maybe I want to capture some of that simplicity. I haven't really changed since I was a kid; in a way I'm stuck at the age of ten. I'm very animated: I'm fidgety and I don't shut up or give in. I even look like a cartoon character – I'm thin with a big, ferrety smile. I like that.'

Cox also likes the way a cartoonist's pen can describe Minnie Mouse's shoe in a few strokes, or Popeye's boot with a blob of ink. He works at bringing that simplicity into his own collections. Minnie the muse has inspired several exaggerated designs for doll-like shoes topped with rounded, stylized bows. He says, 'I like the round friendliness of a Disney cartoon shoe. It's encouraging rather than alienating.' He used the same idea for his 'dolly' shoe, a platypus-toed Mary-Jane finished with an outsized buckle. Here he scales up a child's shoe, an idea used again for his 'little-boy' men's sandals.

In a less obvious way, Cox's simpler styles owe their purity to this graphic art. He almost consciously edits his work so that it applies to the rules followed by the great studios of Disney and Hanna Barbera. He is known for snub-toed and rounded shoes and, in terms of detail, the 'one big idea instead of several small ones'. The design process mostly becomes an exercise in subtraction rather than addition. In the same way that the shoe last is pared and honed, so too is the design itself.

By creating Minnie's shoes, and trimming sandals with an overgrown buckle, Cox shows us an impish sense of humour and irreverence which is unusual, to say the least, in the designer sphere. It is an antidote to the fashion industry's serious-mindedness; in short, a great joke.

'THE JETSONS' SHOE
Spring/summer 1989

**The Jetsons, a space-age cartoon family, were the inspiration for this shoe; the geometric clear plastic panel re-creates the windscreen on their spaceship.**

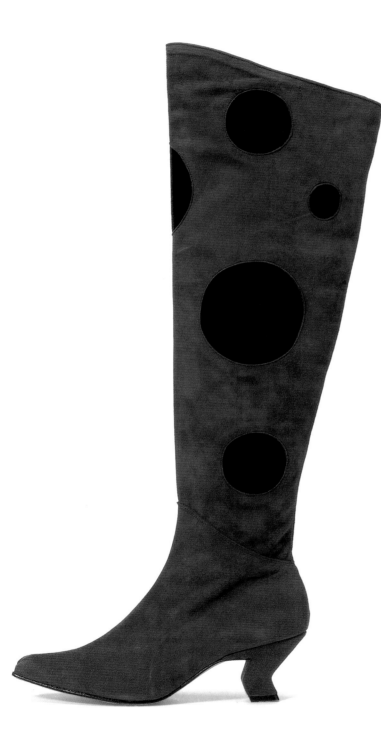

## POLKA-DOT BOOT
Autumn/winter 1988

**Graphic discs of suede are inset into a knee-boot. Cox works at bringing a cartoonist's simplicity into his designs.**

## 'COOKIE' BOOT
1980s

**Suede boots are shaped with half-moon cutouts to make them look like 'a cookie with a bite taken out of it'.**

'DOLLY' SHOES
1986

**Platypus-toed flatties are trimmed with giant, child-like buckles to give the feel of a doll's shoe.**

33

# Plastic fantastic

**P**ATRICK COX LOVES plastic in the way that kids love plasticine. With it he plays with shapes and contours which cannot be achieved with leather and fabric. 'It's a great medium. It's modern and democratic. It's also playful. It releases you from a thousand constraints. When I lived in Nigeria, everyone who wasn't in business wore plastic shoes – incredibly vivid shoes that couldn't have been made in anything else.' Colour is one of many reasons why Cox has pushed the development of plastics in footwear. His most popular styles to date are vivid jellies: kitsch sandals moulded into rubbery styles. These are designs to brighten up the day, to bring a smile to people's faces.

This combination of humour and unpretentiousness is the reason why Cox has ignored the usual snobberies attached to plastic. 'It has always been an alternative to leather shoes. At their best they're cheap with fake leather detailing. Mine rejoice in the fact that they're plastic…There's no pretend stitching or styling to suggest, even for a second, that they are anything other than what they are.'

Cox has introduced a lightweight thong for men and women, moulded from indestructible plastic. 'These are very ergonomic shoes. We use plastic for designs that couldn't be done in leather – sometimes transparent, sometimes sharply sculptured. I love the fact that these shoes are a product of the late twentieth century. They're spat out of the machine – it's an act of pure engineering, more like making a car.' Despite appearances, production is still a skilled process. 'Engineers work on lathes and moulds to catch my ideas and it's important they get it right first time. Unlike the process for my leather work, you don't get a second try – the moulds are incredibly expensive.'

One jelly design, which bears a miniature tourist attraction buried in the water-filled heel,

'JELLY WELLY'
Autumn/winter 1996

**Sleek and slender, the essential city boot is moulded from plastic. 'It's a great medium. It's modern and democratic.'**

Cox's ergonomic thong flies across the advertising image. 'We use plastic for designs that couldn't be done in leather... I love the fact that these shoes are a product of the late twentieth century.'

PATRICK ❦ COX

has become a collector's item. In the style of a snow-shaker, the scene is bathed in a rain of glitter when the wearer walks. While Cox was researching this idea, he spent days trying to explain the concept to a South American factory which produces six million jellies every month. 'I went to the centre of London and bought those double-decker buses and miniature black cabs, while my friends went out to tourist stores next to the Statue of Liberty and the Eiffel Tower to pick up trinkets. I arrived in Brazil and dumped them on the table at the manufacturer's. They looked at me as if I was nuts. They were obviously thinking, "What on earth have we got ourselves into?". For a while they couldn't get a grip on what I was saying. Without fluent Portuguese I couldn't explain that the Eiffel Tower actually went in the heel…'

Cox wanted to make a tourist jelly for Brazil, too, but there was a hitch. 'We wanted to use the famous Christ the Redeemer statue in Rio. The manufacturer had to explain to me that the concept of walking on a pair of Christs wouldn't go down too well in a Catholic country.'

JELLY WEDGE
Spring/summer 1996

**Wash-clean, beach-happy footwear. Cox's plastic mules parody expensive leather styles but glory in the fact that they are virtually indestructible.**

EIFFEL TOWER
JELLY
Spring/summer 1996

**When Cox explained that
he wanted to put trinkets
into the heels of his jellies,
the Brazilian manufacturer
thought he was 'nuts'. His
walking tourist attractions
became a bestseller, and
are now collector's items.**

37

## TV addict

**W**HEN COX MOVED to Britain he had a problem. There were only four television channels and he didn't understand the chatty tradition of British radio. 'People just talked all the time. Where was the music?' Cox had been brought up immersed in North American culture with its delivery of 24-hour entertainment; he admits that this terminally reduced his concentration span to the length of a four-minute record or half-hour TV programme.

Television has influenced every corner of what Cox does, and who he is. Even though he is Anglo-Canadian, his accent belongs somewhere on the western seaboard of the United States. Cox learned his language from a screen in the basement of his parents' house. 'I was a TV kid from the start. When dad came home from his trips I'd hardly look up from the set. I'd get home from school, switch it on and disengage just like every other kid in the Western world. I was just a North American teenager… During the Seventies, TV was a whole chunk of your life. Also, in Edmonton it's so cold outside that for months at a time you don't get out much.'

Rhoda Morgenstern, actress Valerie Harper's over-anxious New Yorker, is one of several TV heroines to have a Patrick Cox shoe last named after her. 'My references are always more about TV and video than about the movies – I don't know Bette Davis' filmography off by heart, for instance.' When he talks about the 'Rhoda', a chunky platform reminiscent of 1976 (the year Harper won the Outstanding Lead Comedy Actress award for her televisual alter ego), Cox discusses the inspiration as though she is probably alive and

SEAMED
KNEE-BOOT
Autumn/winter 1996

**Inspired by Charlie's Angels, the knee-boot is squared off and cut from Seventies-style beige leather.**

## WHIPS SANDAL
Spring/summer 1997

**Chunkiest of all, the flared heel elevates a square and bare sandal.**

## WEDGE SANDAL
Spring/summer 1997

**The wedge is highlighted with a double wave of silver leather on a style that should have been worn by Rhoda Morgenstern, even if it wasn't.**

39

SEAMED BOOT
Autumn/winter 1996

**Inspired by Starsky and Hutch's pal Huggy Bear; Seventies hip is sewn into the flat, squared ankle boot for guys.**

still living in Minneapolis. He pauses for a moment to work out if Mary Tyler Moore deserves her own last, but he thinks not; 'She's too demure; kind of ladylike Sixties'.

Rhoda has her place, but Cox becomes frantic at the thought of Charlie's Angels. Waving his arms and shaking his head as though lost in a mist of Farrah's hairspray, he says, 'I was totally obsessed by Farrah, Kate and Kelly. The styling was genius – it is still genius today.' Cox now owns a lock of Farrah Fawcett's airy blonde hair and when he sits down to design she is still at the front of his mind. 'It's all invented memory. I don't pull out cuttings and think, "What a great sandal," but I'm tuned in to the mood of what they were doing. It's about remembering the way she would pull a pistol out of that tiny clutch [bag] which had this amazing ability to swallow huge things. I think of a heel she could have run in. It's a flash of white leather.'

The 'TV memory' is all-embracing. 'Dukes of Hazzard, Starsky and Hutch, Dynasty, Star Trek: they are all programmed in my head; the way Krystal Carrington's hair flipped and Joan Collins's make-up stayed just-so through a fight.' Now Cox heads a £20 million business he doesn't have too much time to get his TV fix. He suffers from 'information anxiety' and claims, 'I need to be bombarded with information. When I'm staying at a hotel, MTV or CNN chatters away in the corner. I say to Fabbrizio, "Oh look, it's 32 degrees in Riyadh today," and he says, "So what?". He just doesn't get it – for me it's a quick hit.'

### BROGUE COURT
Autumn/winter 1996

**A squared-off loafer is raised on a chunky heel.**

### SUEDE WEDGE MARY-JANE
Autumn/winter 1996

**A classic flat-soled wedge with a Seventies feel, using colour-variant suede.**

PATRICK COX

### COLOUR-VARIANT MARY-JANE
Autumn/winter 1996

**Another Charlie's Angels staple, the Mary-Jane is a glamour shoe. 'The styling [on Charlie's Angels] was genius – it's still genius today.'**

41

'WHEN I MET Ian Schrager a few years ago I told him that my biggest regret in life was that I was too young ever to go to Studio 54.' Schrager was one half of the partnership (with Steve Rubell) that ran Manhattan's infamous Seventies club, where waiters wore white satin jockstraps and the playboy and playgirl customers not much more. Columnist Jean Rook described it as 'a seething pot of smoking, writhing and dancing bodies, lit up with a massive man-in-the-moon snorting cocaine from a spoon and by strobes that make girls' eyes hang out of their heads like their boobs tumble out of their shirts.' It's that element of unbridled glamour and unsurpassed hedonism which so appeals to Cox.

The only thing the 12-year-old Cox had in common with Studio 54 regulars at that time was a passion for Donna Summer's disco anthems. 'That beat was a constant in my life. When I was 14 I camped out to see Abba when they arrived in Alberta. Annafrida was wearing lace-up suede boots. Very Scandinavian, and very important for me, as it turns out, since there are echoes of them in the Wannabe.'

TV, as so often before, played a formative role. 'I'd watch American Bandstand in the basement. It was there I saw Blondie, Grace [Jones] and the rest of them for the first time. I remember the dancers; one wore a pair of boots with teddy bears in the heels. I dreamed of going to New York to be a part of it all.'

As he reviews his work, the Cox archive sounds more like a discography, with the 1997 Dragon Boot inspired by rock cock Gene Simmons ('Lick It Up') and rock chick Pat Benatar ('Hit Me With Your Best Shot'), and the Blondie ('Heart of Glass') upright heel and last. It's probably just as well that Cox didn't feel able to attend the Bay City Rollers' Edmonton date. The idea of being the only boy in a sea of screaming teenies kept him at home, so we will have to live without the Eric Faulkner ('Bye Bye Baby') platform boot.

During Madonna's 1990 'Blond Ambition' tour, Cox realized a long-held dream when he presented the singer with a pair of custom-made pumps. (Since then she has become a paying customer.) Unlike the true 'fan', however, Cox does not believe in idol worship and separates the idea of fantasy icon from the living reality. 'Icons and fantasies should remain that way. They're just people, whereas the image is so much more.'

CHAIN-MAIL
BEATLE BOOT'
Autumn/winter 1991

**The squared leather boot is based on the classic Beatle boot but given Cox's touch with chain-mail insets.**

'DISCO T-BAR'
Autumn/winter 1996

The disco sheen of
metallic leather adds to
the feel of Stephanie's
dance shoes in *Saturday
Night Fever*.

'PRINCE' SHOE
Autumn/winter 1980s

Inspired by Prince, the
purple crucifix court wears
a cross and chain across
the upper. Cox says of the
rock icons who inspire him,
'They're just people,
whereas the image is so
much more.'

43

## LEOPARD METALLIC SANDAL
Spring/summer 1998

Designed for pleasure, the leopard sandal was inspired by the New Wave hedonism of the late Seventies.

## 'BLONDIE' MULE
Spring/summer 1998

The spirit of platinum rock goddess Debbie Harry lives, in a pair of high-heel, high-shine mules.

44

## 'ZIP' BOOT
Spring/summer 1998

**The rock chick boot: Pat Benatar was the inspiration for this biker boot scarred with silver zips.**

## CUFF MULE
Spring/summer 1998

**A satin boot is lined with gold leather and cut down to make the ultimate in disco-diva footwear.**

'I LOVE THE UNION JACK. It's iconic. It's the most beautiful flag and stands for so much.' Not the words of the Queen, but Patrick Cox on one of the reasons why he has settled in Britain. 'I'm an incredible monarchist. I put it down to being a history buff and coming from a place where anything made in the Fifties is an antique. When I arrived in Britain I buried myself in the history. Architecturally I prefer France – hence the fleur de lys on my label and my passion for any French furniture between Louis XIV and Napoleon – but I dream about the Queen all the time and get emotional when I hear "Pomp and Circumstance". I adore Princess Margaret because she's so naughty; and the Queen Mother is just, well, marvellous.'

Patrick Cox was anything but a reluctant colonist. 'I have a deep respect for the Queen. I've lived throughout the Commonwealth and virtually every coin I've ever used has had her head on it. America feels soulless by comparison.' Cox regrets that he must now spend six months of the year away from Britain, mostly in Italy. He misses the British people, whom he likens to the national canine symbol: 'I love the bulldog because its strength is in its character, and that's how I see the British personality.' He also admires the diversity he finds in Britain. 'Nowhere else can you walk onto the street and see a hundred nationalities living together without being swallowed up by the whole – like they are in America, where the state is overwhelming. I live here for the people.'

Stylistically, Cox sees the British experience as central to his work, and no more so than with the monarchy. 'To me, the Queen and the Queen Mother's style is solid; it's something like that smell you experience when your grandmother hugs you. The matching handbag; the

ADVERTISING
IMAGE
1996

**The bulldog and the Union Jack are enduring symbols of the country that Cox now calls home.**

**A quintessential London style inspired by the Youthquake cult of the Sixties.**

TARTAN COURT
Autumn/winter 1994

**A classic court shape receives the Caledonian treatment with tartan cloth.**

## WINKLE-PICKER BOOT
### Autumn/winter 1995

**Cox makes the Sixties Chelsea boot his own by giving it a heavier sole, a nod towards what he calls 'solid cobbling'.**

head-to-toe colour that's bright enough to be spotted ten miles away; the design of their clunky, slightly platformed shoes… My dream is to do shoes for the Queen.'

British contemporary tribal history is also a source for Cox. 'Mods and punks have had a mind-boggling impact on fashion history, in the same way that black teenagers in the US have done. Clothes have become a way of inventing a tribal language – working-class kids tend to design through necessity. In Italy style is always about looking older, but here it's about being young. I want to live in a place where things start, and to me most things begin in Britain.'

Cox cites the British tradition of solid cobbling as a primary inspiration. That said, he is obliged to manufacture in Italy, the centre of the shoe world. 'The Marches can be a brutal place but there is a concentration of speed and effort there,' says Cox. 'If I didn't have to turn to Italy for the craftsmanship, I would certainly spend more time in Britain. At this time, though, British manufacturing still isn't geared to producing a flexible and efficient system.'

## PUNCHED SLING-BACK
### Spring/summer 1996

'The Queen Mother's style is solid... the matching handbag, the head-to-toe colour that's bright enough to be seen ten miles away...' Cox celebrates the Queen Mum in his own way in a pair of sturdy sling-back sandals.

## KITTEN HEEL
### Autumn/winter 1995

The Kings Road shoe is very close to its Sixties original as worn by Chelsea girls: sharp, pert and cool. 'In Italy style is always about looking older, but here it's about being young.'

'WHEN MOST TODDLERS were developing a crush on their mother's high heels, I was into the trophy footwear worn by businessmen in Nigeria.' Black and white snakeskin became Cox's own particular distinctive fetish so whenever it's an appropriate option, he uses it.

Black and white says a lot about Cox and the diversity, and sometimes conflicts, in his work, and not simply because it is a tonal theme that recurs throughout his shoes. 'Until the mid-Nineties every bestselling shoe of mine was a black and white one. It's a subconscious detail. Black and white to me is about graphics; it is clean, modern and ultimately the purest combination… I don't see myself as a colourist [so] using black and white is the purest way of not dealing with that specification.'

In 1986 Cox designed a pair of white Oxfords for women with the laces and welt delineated in black, making them look as though he had taken a marker to them. In the same year, a pair of black backless ghillies threaded with white laces counterpointed John Flett's collection of draped, deconstructed jersey. In 1992 the outline of plain black sandals was picked out with leather strips to imitate the white dashes of running stitch. The reasoning and geometric quality to all of this work is, perhaps, a reminder that Cox was always good at mathematics.

## CUFF EVENING SHOE
Autumn/winter 1991

**A satin evening shoe mimics a dress cuff, using a jet button to suggest the cufflink.**

## PUNCHED MULE
Spring/summer 1992

***Opposite*: A black leather mule is delineated with white 'top-stitched' leather strips to mimic the edge of camera film.**

## 'WICKED WITCH' GHILLIE
Spring/summer 1994

**Brogued Edwardian walking shoes; the black and white theme throws the punch design into stark relief.**

'PIED DE POULE'
Spring/summer 1996

**Houndstooth printed patent leather is thrown into relief with the use of black and white on a sling-back and classic court. Cox sees it as 'clean, modern and ultimately the purest combination'.**

ZIG-ZAG T-BAR
Spring/summer 1996

**'Black and white is to me about graphics.' Here, a white zig-zag cuts across the toe of a T-bar shoe with cartoon-like clarity.**

## PYTHON BOOT
### Autumn/winter 1995

**The winkle-picker boot is cut from Cox's favourite material: black-and-white python. It was a passion born in Africa where the young Cox was at ground level with the trophy footwear of Nigerian businessmen.**

## ROLL-TONGUE
### For John Galliano, 1987

**This two-tone shoe became a hit in 1987, after no fewer than three pop stars wore it to the same chat show in the space of a week.**

In 1987 Cox produced a two-tone shoe for John Galliano, called the 'Roll-Tongue'. He had already proved his credentials as the 'Ferragamo for the MTV generation' with his toe-capped DMs which had become, in Vivienne Westwood's words, 'the most copied shoes of the decade'. The Roll-Tongue shot to TV stardom when it appeared on the feet of three different pop stars on Terry Wogan's chat show – all in the space of one week. Boy George and a member of Wet Wet Wet were followed by Elton John, at which point Wogan touched Elton's Roll-Tongue and asked him to 'tell me about these'. A pair is now in the Twentieth Century Dress Collection at the Victoria and Albert Museum.

At the same time, two other designs by Patrick Cox were both regularly featured in glossy magazines: a woman's style that mimicked Coco Chanel's classic two-tone pump, and a man's T-bar sandal with black toe caps and white body. Cox now sees a thread which binds these moments together through the 15 years he has been designing shoes. 'Black and white is a purifying combination, one that prepares us for a time when we will be dominated by colour again. Op-art came before the antiquey browns of the Seventies; 2-Tone before the costume drama of the early Eighties. These mid-Eighties incarnations were like a precursor to a turn-of-the-decade explosion of colour. It can almost be thought of as a neutral which cleans our palate.'

There are also other, more practical, reasons for choosing the monochromatic two-tone. 'Being a shoe designer, you have to propose – you can't dictate an entire outfit in the way a fashion designer can. You have to take your product and offer it as an accessory to the wider image. Black and white is the strongest proposition. It's eye-catching, but it's neutral – it works with all colours.

TWO-TONE
LACE-UP
Autumn/winter 1994

**Sharpened toes on a pair of exaggerated Oxfords. 'Black and white is a purifying combination, one that prepares us for a time when we will be dominated by colour again.'**

# God is in the details

'I'M A FASTENINGS FETISHIST. My magpie eye collects details – anything that catches my attention – and I apply them to my shoes'. A queenly diamanté buckle; an upper of delicate woven leather or cotton lace; an embroidered oriental dragon winding its way up a satin boot – all have caught Cox's attention. For him, detail is what makes the shoe special, particularly with the Patrick Cox line. Sometimes the details are modest: a woven raffia thong sandal in memory of a summer holiday, or a toggle from a Beatnik duffel coat. At other times they are precious: the sterling silver heels worked for a pair of suede pumps in 1988, the winter boots trimmed with a cascade of Mongolian lambskin, the embroidered dragon – which was originally sampled using hand embroidery at a cost of £1,000 per boot. Whichever, Cox's shoes are more usually identifiable by their restraint. 'It's easy to overload shoes but the essence should be about one good idea. A beautiful buckle on a nice clean shoe is probably the best example.'

The details have not always been so subtle. Thick steel plates were screwed onto a squared boot-toe in 1988 in a feat of mechanical engineering. Large, beaten gold buttons decorated some otherwise well-mannered almond-toed shoes and boots for women in 1992. On occasions, especially when the shape

EMBROIDERED LACE-UP
Spring/summer 1993

**Decorative embroidery is applied to a plain, soft men's nubuck shoe.**

'CHAIN REACTION'
1988

**An overtly sexy detail: the plain black court is given a chain-mail skirt to cover its stiletto heel.**

## PETAL ANKLE STRAP
Spring/summer 1997

**A dainty summer shoe is trimmed with a giant satin couture flower. 'If it's worthy of being there in the first place, it has to be perfect.'**

## SILVER-HEELED PUMP
Spring/summer 1988

**Twisted heels are formed in solid silver for an otherwise understated suede pump.**

## LACE SANDAL
Autumn/winter 1997

**The peep-toe sandal is dressed with delicate lingerie lace over metallic leather.**

## 'DRAGON' BOOT
Autumn/winter 1997

**The spectacular Chinese satin boot was initially embroidered by hand; customers were seduced by the special detail and shops sold out within a week – despite the £650 price tag.**

of the shoe is too well-behaved, Cox exagger-
ates the detail to drive the irony home. He will
take the bamboo handbag handle popularized
by Gucci and forge it into an entire heel in an
irreverent memorial to American society
doyennes of the Fifties.

At the Cox headquarters on Sloane Street,
the first thing a visitor encounters is a long
stainless steel staircase lit from the side. Shine has
as much impact on Cox's work, whether it is
gold leather or satin used to highlight a basic
loafer shape, or his famous 'Chain Reaction'
courts, with their heels secreted behind a chain-
mail skirt. 'The art to designing good accessories
is to work with lots of materials, and to apply
new ones just when you've thought there
can't be anything new out there. It was difficult
when I was manufacturing in Britain because
for three years I was told, "there is only one
buckle". So I had to use the same buckle over
and over again – which was somewhat limiting.
A shoe and its detail have to be relevant to the
time they are designed in. A few seasons ago we
did a belt, the buckle of which was a butterfly
picked out in diamanté. The motif was remem-
bered from the Seventies but wasn't heavy, it had
to work for the Nineties.'

The flower is a recurring motif. Cox says, 'A
lot of our flowers come from LCT in Paris, a
company that supplies the couture houses.
Quality is vital to detail; if it's worthy of being
there in the first place, it has to be perfect.' To
make that detail his own, Cox adds his touch: he
will take a couture rose and sprinkle it with
sequins, like 'the disco dust that made the flower
in Donna Summer's hair glitter'.

ZIG-ZAG
SOLED SHOE
1988

Cox, the self-styled
'fastenings fetishist',
borrows the briefcase
clasp for a sporty shoe.

BUTTERFLY THONGS
Spring/summer 1997

Stylized butterflies garnish a pair of
simple thong sandals.

A black satin boot is
given the cuff treatment,
using two jet buttons as
cufflinks.

MONGOLIAN
BOOT
1990s

A swathe of Mongolian
lambskin drapes a suede
boot in memory of Abba's
tour of Canada in the
Seventies.

LONDON FASHION WEEK, 26 September 1997; Blondie, Grace Jones and the B-52s give megawatt blasts from the sound system in a gigantic warehouse studio. The audience, well-lubricated with vodka, is watching a mocked-up fashion shoot which includes wind machine, lights and Mohican hair by Sam McKnight. On a raised platform, Helena Christensen poses in a stretch silk leopard-print dress. On her feet are a pair of futuristic fuchsia chromed clogs. It's a heady presentation with a New Wave feel to it; the colours are supernova-bright; the heels are high, higher or highest, and Cox knows that his clean and lean clothing line is now ready to be shown off.

Nowadays, Patrick Cox is more than a label on a shoe. Diversification crowded his biography from the mid-Nineties onwards. From the success of his mainline collection he moved to consolidate the Wannabe range. In 1995 he added clothes and leather accessories to the line. Then in the following year he made what seemed to be the least likely addition to the list of products bearing his logo: a scooter. But even that has a place in the world of Patrick Cox. 'A scooter is fashion friendly – you don't need all the full motorcycle leather gear – you can ride one wearing a suit,' Cox declares.

'I'd seen a friend's silver Vespa, and wanted one – it looked good but it weighed a ton. Then I saw that Italjet had just brought out the Velocifero, a retro-styled model that looked like a cross between an old Vespa and a Lambretta, and I had to have it! I used it around London at the same time as Anna Sui put one on the runway. Journalists wanted to do the "scooter story", and since I was the only designer riding

one I was interviewed about it, and photographed on it, again and again.

'The scooter manufacturer ended up finding a British distributor, Frontier Motorcycles. They called me up and said, "We feel this is because of you – would you like to do something with us?" I said that I wanted to customize mine with a python seat. In turn they asked if I wanted just one or if I'd like to do a limited edition. Since I didn't want to be the only person riding a scooter with my name on it, I agreed. When the Wannabe scooter came out people would walk up to me and say, "Patrick Cox?" and I wasn't sure if they were referring to me or the scooter.'

Cox is funny, Cox is clever, Cox runs his company as an extension of himself – a hyperactive ideas machine that does not know the meaning of 'can't'. 'I'm not shallow, but I'm not at all introspective. I don't torture myself over what my next move is going to be, I just go out and make that thing happen.'

'That thing' has meant going global: by the end of 1998 there will be 25 Patrick Cox shops dotted around the world, in particular around the Pacific Rim – a far cry from the days of customizing DMs in King's Cross.

But Cox is careful about what he attaches his name to. 'We've spent ten years building up an image and it can be destroyed in one fell swoop. I feel that we've now got a thriving company which also has credibility – the kind of credibility a big American designer would pay an advertising agency millions to create.' There is one last object Cox wants to customize: his own jet, decorated with a python interior and a sound system that would play the music of Donna Summer and his other disco inspirations to the heavens. 'We'll see,' he says. 'We'll see.'

**1963**
Born in Edmonton, Alberta, Canada.

**1983**
Moves to London to follow course in footwear design at Cordwainers Technical College.

**1984**
Whilst at college, designs and produces footwear for Vivienne Westwood's autumn/winter1984/85 collection and Bodymap's 'Half World' show.

**1985**
Graduates from Cordwainers, and immediately sets up own company designing, producing and selling footwear.

**1986**
Designs footwear for the John Galliano 'Fallen Angels' spring/summer show. Launches Patrick Cox label collection for spring/summer 1987; thereafter produces two collections a year. Meanwhile, continues to work on footwear for various designers including Alistair Blair, John Flett, Richmond/ Cornejo, Workers for Freedom, Anna Sui, Richard James and John Galliano.

**1988**
Patrick Cox production moves to Italy.

**1991**
Opens first shop at 8 Symons Street, London SW3.

**1993**
Launch of the Patrick Cox Wannabe collection for autumn/winter 1993/94.

**1994**
First Patrick Cox shop opens in Paris at 62 rue Tiquetonne, 2ᵉ. Launch of first clothing collection, for spring/summer 1995. Also launch of PC diffusion range. Wins Accessory Designer of the Year at the British Fashion Awards.

## 1995

Opens first shop in USA, at 702 Madison Avenue, New York, and second London shop, at 129 Sloane Street, London SW1. Also opens international headquarters at 30 Sloane Street. Wins Accessory Designer of the Year award for the second year running.

## 1997

First catwalk show, showing the Patrick Cox clothing collection and held during London Fashion Week.

## 1998

Launch of Patrick Cox gold scooter for spring/summer 1998.

## 1996

Launch of the Patrick Cox Wannabe black and white python-seated scooter. The Twentieth Century Fashion Department at London's Victoria and Albert Museum acquires a pair of Eiffel Tower jelly sandals. Customizes headphones, portable phone and TV for Sony, using signature python skin.

# Index

# Acknowledgements

The publishers wish to thank Patrick Cox and Antonia Myles-White for their kind assistance with all aspects of this book.

*Photographic credits*
Page 6: courtesy Patrick Cox
Page 8: courtesy Patrick Cox/photo Kevin Davies
Page 9: courtesy Patrick Cox/photos Regan Cameron
Page 10 right: courtesy Patrick Cox
Page 12 left: courtesy Patrick Cox/Solid Bond Productions
Page 12 right: courtesy Patrick Cox/photo Inez van Lamsweerde
Page 14 inset: Niall McInerny
Page 17 inset: Niall McInerny
Page 20 inset: Rex Features
Page 25 left: courtesy Patrick Cox
Page 35: courtesy Patrick Cox
Page 38 inset: Rex Features
Page 42 inset top: Rex Features
Page 42 bottom: Rex Features
Page 46 inset: Rex Features
Page 46 right: courtesy Patrick Cox
Page 58: courtesy Patrick Cox
Page 59: courtesy Patrick Cox
Page 60 top: courtesy Patrick Cox; centre: courtesy Patrick Cox/photo Kevin Davies; bottom: courtesy Patrick Cox/photo Inez van Lamsweerde
Page 61 bottom left: courtesy Sony; right: courtesy Patrick Cox/photos Dan Len; other pictures courtesy Patrick Cox

All other photography by Guy Ryecart